WILMINGTON PUBLIC LIBRARY DISTRICT
P9-DFY-600

21st Century Skills INNOVATION LIBRARY

UNOFFICIAL GUIDES

MINDSTORMS: Level 3

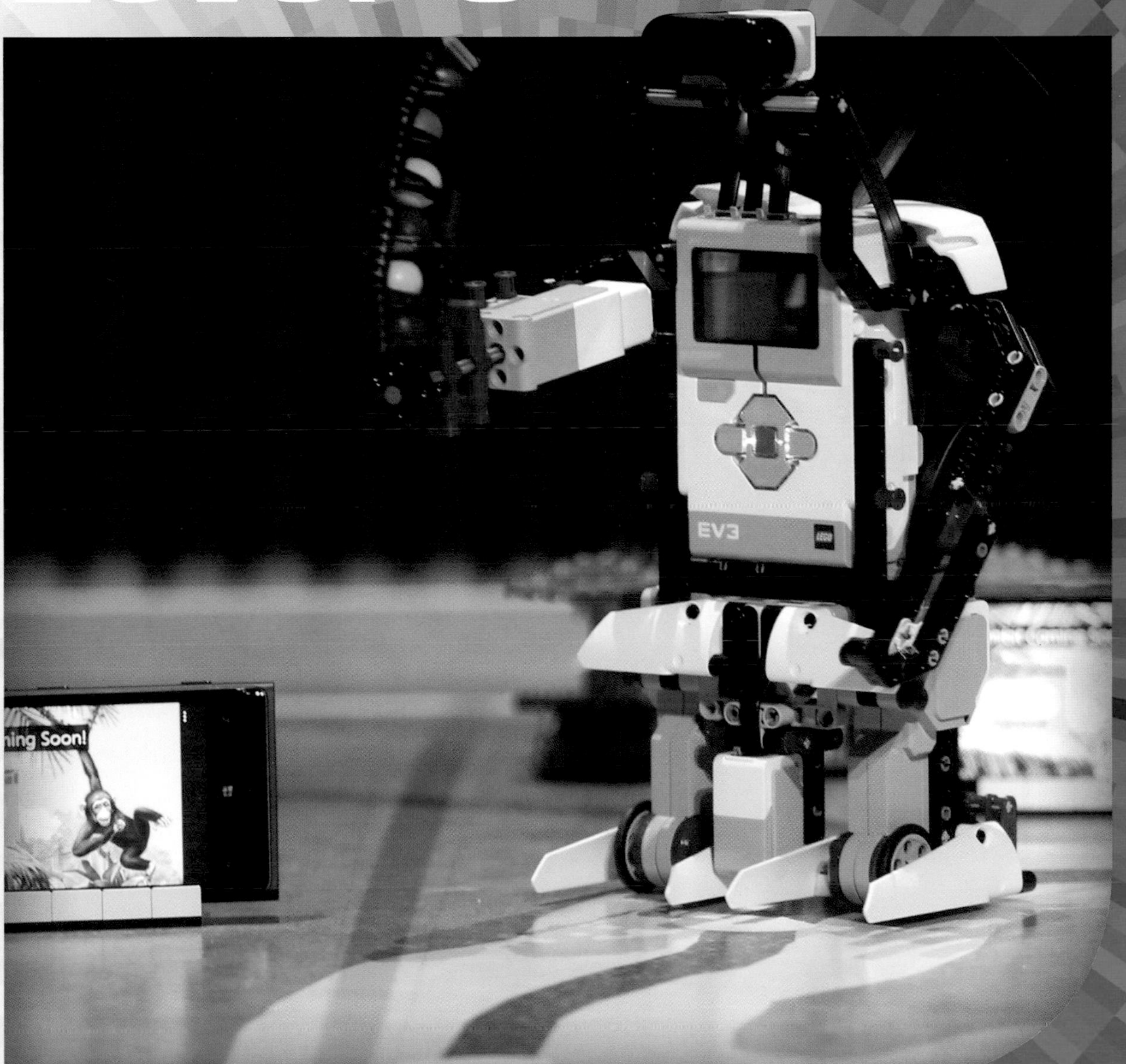

CHERRY LAKE PUBLISHING • ANN ARBOR, MICHIGAN

by Rena Hixon

A Note to Adults: Please review the instructions for the activities in this book before allowing children to do them. Be sure to help them with any activities you do not think they can safely complete on their own.

A Note to Kids: Be sure to ask an adult for help with these activities when you need it. Always put your safety first!

Published in the United States of America by Cherry Lake Publishing
Ann Arbor, Michigan
www.cherrylakepublishing.com

Reading Adviser: Marla Conn, Read With Me Now
Photo Credits: Cover and page 1, ©AP Images; page 5, ©Robert Mandel/Shutterstock; pages 17, 20, and 24, Rena Hixon; page 22, ©Beloborod/Shutterstock; page 29, Érre/tinyurl.com/oa4efw6/CC BY-SA 2.0

Library of Congress Cataloging-in-Publication Data
Names: Hixon, Rena, author.
Title: Mindstorms. Level 3 / by Rena Hixon.
Description: Ann Arbor, Michigan : Cherry Lake Publishing, [2016] | Series: 21st century skills innovation library. Unofficial guides | Audience: Grades 4 to 6.- | Includes bibliographical references and index.
Identifiers: LCCN 2015034877| ISBN 9781634705264 (lib. bdg.) | ISBN 9781634706469 (pbk.) | ISBN 9781634705868 (pdf) | ISBN 9781634707060 (ebook)
Subjects: LCSH: LEGO Mindstorms toys–Juvenile literature. | Robotics–Juvenile literature. | Computer programming–Juvenile literature. | Detectors–Juvenile literature.
Classification: LCC TJ211.2 .H486 2016 | DDC 629.8/92–dc23 LC record available at http://lccn.loc.gov/2015034877

Cherry Lake Publishing would like to acknowledge the work of The Partnership for 21st Century Skills. Please visit *www.p21.org* for more information.

Printed in the United States of America
Corporate Graphics
January 2016

21st Century Skills **INNOVATION LIBRARY**

Contents

Chapter 1

Understanding Programming Concepts

If you're reading this book, you probably already know about some of the incredible things you can do with Lego Mindstorms. You may have even built some Mindstorms robots yourself. Hopefully you know how the different sensors are used, how to create simple programs, and how to use the EV3 programmable brick. If not, you should start by reading *Unofficial Guides: Mindstorms Level 1* and *Level 2*. Then come back to this book once you're ready!

The EV3 software is extremely powerful. It can be used to create robots far more complex than the ones we made in previous books. This book will focus on creating programs that will allow your robots to do more than one thing at a time. For example, in the previous books, we made a robot that could follow a line and a robot that would stop before running into walls. But we can also write a program that tells a robot how to do both of those things. In addition, we will look at some **icons** in the EV3 software that you can use to accomplish some more complex things with your robot.

Let's start by reviewing the basics of Mindstorms programming. We will use the same robot we built for the activities in Level 1 and Level 2.

The programming skills you learn from Mindstorms could help you learn a variety of other programming languages.

In the EV3 software, drag the "Move Tank" icon into a new program. Set it to simply turn the motors on. For now, this will be the only icon in your program. Predict what you think will happen when you run it. Now give it a try. You might have predicted that the motors will run forever. However, either the robot will twitch slightly or nothing will happen at all! To understand why this is, you need to get familiar with some of the common EV3 icons. The green arrow icon is the "Start" icon. This is where every program will start. If you put icons in the programming screen that are not attached to the "Start" icon, nothing will happen.

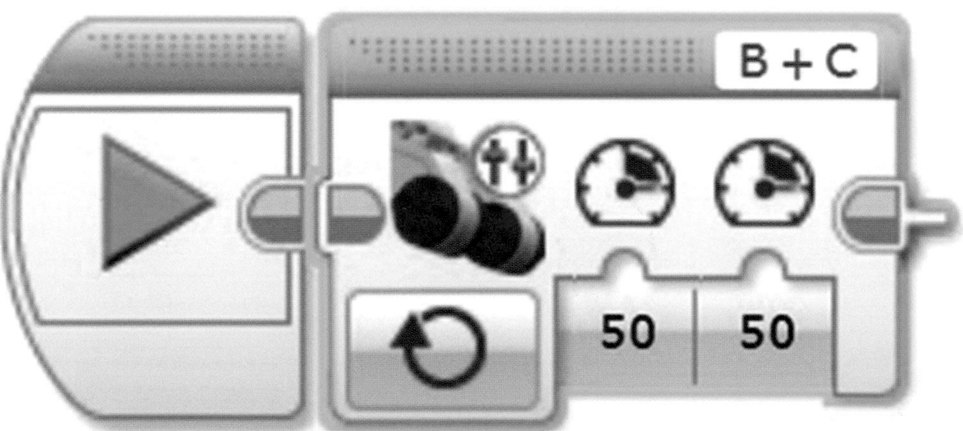

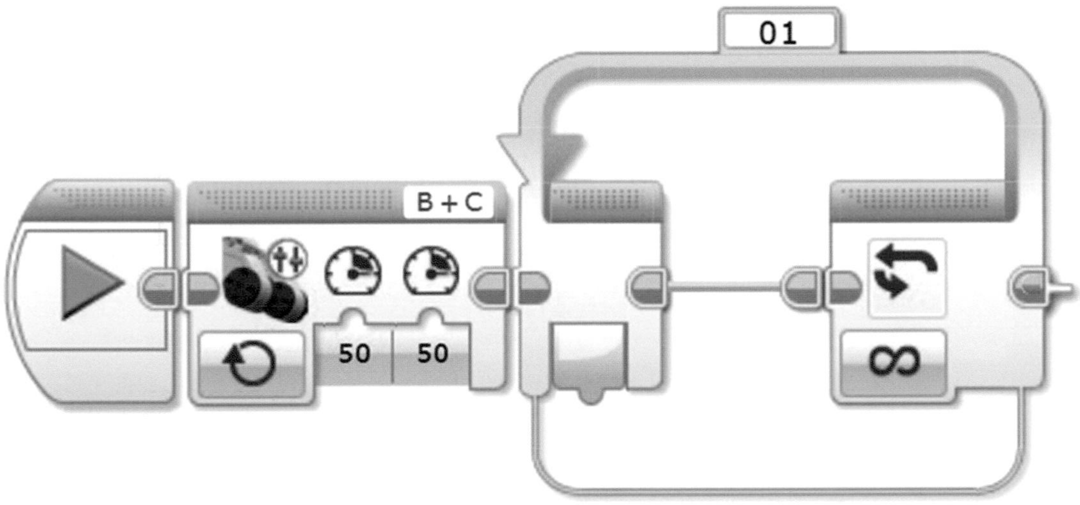

If you want the robot to actually turn on and run forever, then you should add a "Forever" loop to the end of the program. You might think you should put the "Move Tank" icon inside the loop. However, it is more accurate to put the loop after the icon. This way, you are turning on the motors and then telling the program to run forever. If the icon is inside the loop, then you are actually telling it to keep turning on the motors. Understanding these small differences is an important part of figuring out which order your icons should go in.

Another important concept to understand is that icons are executed in the order you see them on-screen. Therefore, if you want your robot to go forward and then make a turn, your icons should be placed in that order.

Another thing you need to understand about programming is that each icon is only **executed** once unless you use a loop to tell it otherwise. For example, many students are confused by the "Switch" icon. This icon checks a condition and then executes one of two actions based on the results. Most students assume that it will keep checking the condition and executing the right action. However, it will only check once unless a loop is around it.

In the following program, the "Switch" icon will be executed once. If it notices that the touch sensor is pressed, the robot will move forward one rotation. If the program is executed and the touch sensor is not pressed, the robot will go backward one rotation. Try running this program to make sure you understand the concept of a "Switch" icon only being executed one time.

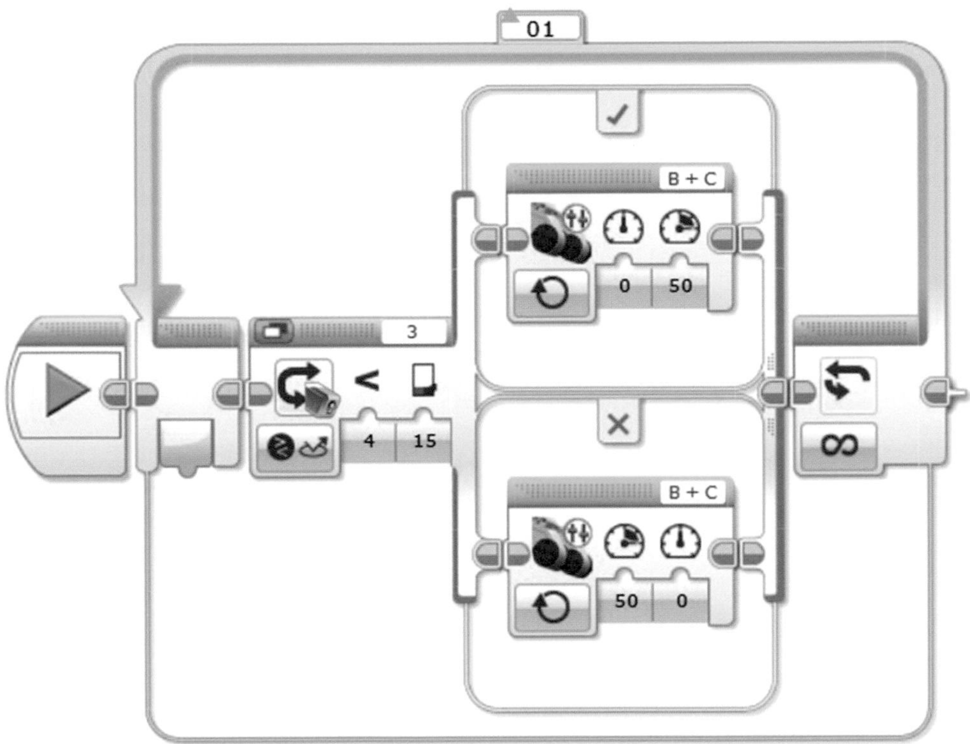

Look back to the line-following program we created in Level 2. This is a good example of a "Switch" icon that needs to execute more than once. The entire program must have a loop around it to keep checking the light value and steering the robot in the right direction. Without this loop, the robot would check the value once and stop.

If you have a loop in your program that has the infinity sign, it will loop forever. You should not expect your program to ever go past that loop.

All About Firmware

Like many electronic devices, the EV3 brick has special built-in software called firmware. Firmware is what allows your programs to run. It also tells the brick how to display information on the screen, how to communicate with sensors, and more. Sometimes the Lego company releases new versions of the EV3 firmware. These versions can add new features and improve the way the EV3 works. You can download them from the Internet and transfer them to your programmable brick much as you do with the programs you create in the EV3 software.

In order to continue your program, you need to get out of the loop.

Let's create a program that instructs our robot to follow a line until it detects an object within 4 inches (10.2 centimeters) in front of it. The robot should stop once it notices the object. Can you figure out how to write a program to accomplish this? In order to try it out, you can use the oval track we created for Level 2. Then set a box or some other object somewhere on top of the line.

Start by making a line-following program like the one in Level 2, then put a loop around it. However, don't use an infinite loop. The loop should only repeat until the ultrasonic sensor notices something less than 4 inches (10.2 cm) away. The last icon in

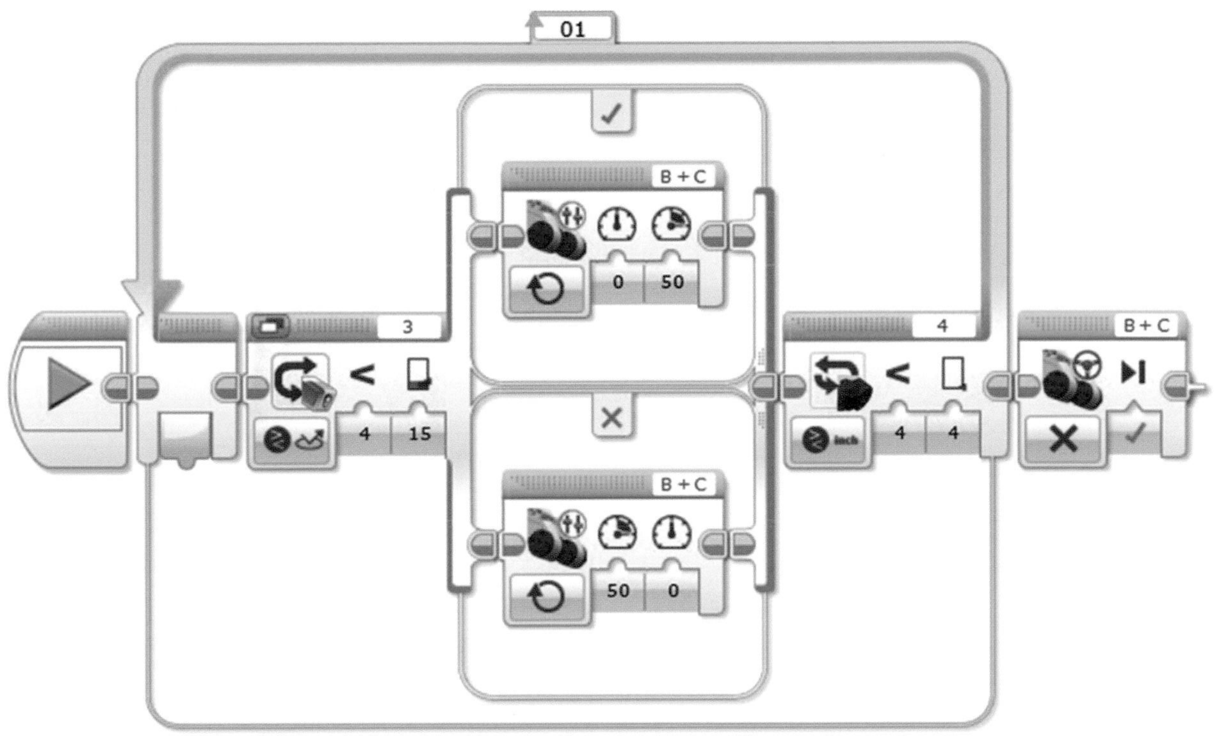

your program should be a "Move Tank" with the motors turned off. For this program to work, you need to have your ultrasonic sensor on the front of your robot.

You are now ready to develop a course of your own and figure out how to put together different program parts to do several tasks. Use tape and poster board to create a long course just like you did for the oval. Add in plenty of curves and turns and obstacles.

Chapter 2

Reading the Light Sensor

As you keep working on more advanced Mindstorms projects, you are bound to run into difficulties from time to time. Luckily, there are some tricks you can use to help **troubleshoot** problems with your programs. The first thing you are going to learn in this chapter is how to display readings from the sensors on the EV3 screen. If you are having problems with a line-following program, for example, you might want to display the values that your robot is reading as it runs the program.

To try this, start with the basic line-following program. Place the "Light Sensor" icon inside the loop, either before or after the "Switch" icon. You will find this and other sensor icons under the yellow tab in the EV3 software. You will also need a "Display" icon. On the "Display" icon, select "Text". The upper left corner of the "Display" icon will say "Mindstorms" when it is first brought into the

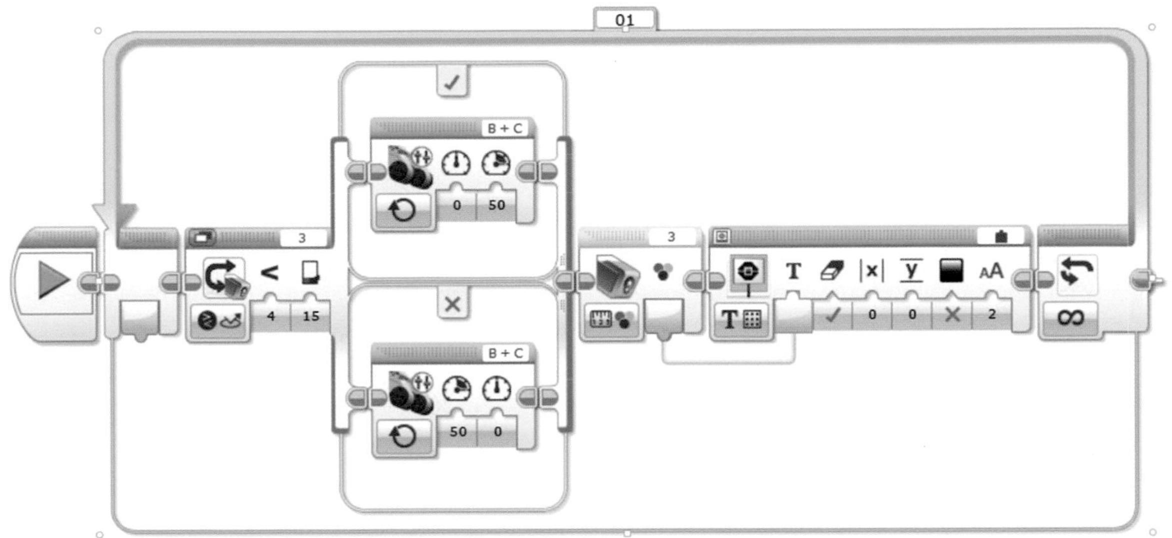

program. Click on that area and select "Wired" instead. Once you have done this, you can pull a yellow "wire" from the "Light Sensor" icon and connect it to the "Display" icon under the "T" tab. On the "Color Sensor" icon, select "Measure–Light Intensity". Remember to set the correct **port** number. When you run the program, you should now be able to see the light values change as your robot moves.

Taking readings from the light sensor is good for more than just troubleshooting. Do you remember making your first line-following program in Level 2? You needed to figure out the exact dark value of the line on your oval and put that information into the

Input and Output

As you work on more advanced programming techniques, you will probably notice that some icons have tabs on the bottom. Those tabs have bumps on either their top or bottom side. If the bump is on the bottom, it means that tab produces an **output**. If the bump is on the top, it means that tab accepts an **input**. For example, the tab on a sensor icon has a bump at the bottom. This is because it can output information to be used by a different icon. The tabs on the "Display" icon are on the top. This means they can accept the information from the sensor icon. To connect an output tab to an input tab, simply click one of them to pull out a yellow "wire" and drag it to the other.

program yourself. Now that you know how to measure values and output them to other icons, you can make your robot do the work for you. Let's program our robot to measure values and use them to follow a line automatically.

Your robot should only read the value once before it begins following the line. This means we need to add some code after the "Start" icon and before the loop. If you put the new code in the loop, the robot would constantly read new values. This is not what we want.

For this program to work correctly, it needs to measure the value from the light sensor and add to it to create the value your robot will use to follow a line. This means you will need to use **variables**. Variables are values that are stored and used within a program. You can use them to make your program calculate math problems.

Click on the red tab. The first icon in this tab is the "Variable" icon. Pull one of these into your program. In the white space at the top of the icon, you are given the option "Add variable". Select this and type in a variable name. The variable name will help you remember what the number in the variable stands for.

The default setting for a "Variable" icon is "Write Numeric" with a value of 0. When working with variables, it is a good idea to start with a 0 variable before adding other icons. This will ensure that the program is starting from scratch when it begins making calculations.

We want to start our math problem with a measurement value from the light sensor, so add a "Light Sensor" icon from the yellow tab. Add it after the 0 variable icon. Now we want our program to add 5 to whatever value the light sensor reads. Go to the red tab and find the "Math" icon. This is the fifth icon under the tab. It has math symbols on it. Bring it into your program and place it after the "Light Sensor" icon. We want to add, so select the + symbol.

To the right of the + symbol, you will see three tabs on the "Math" icon. They are labeled "a", "b", and "=". The "a" and "b" tabs are for inputs, while "=" is an output tab. Connect a wire from the tab of the "Light Sensor" icon to the "a" tab on the "Math" icon. Now select the "b" tab and type "5". This code will send the value from the "Light Sensor" icon to the "Math" icon, then add 5 to it. This creates a new value.

Now we need to turn the value from the "Math" icon into a variable. Add another "Variable" icon to the right of the "Math" icon. Don't forget to name it the same thing you named the last one. Now use a wire to connect the "=" tab from the "Math" icon to the input tab on the new "Variable" icon.

This program segment will start at 0, read the light sensor, and add 5 to the value of the light sensor reading. It will then put the final value back into a variable. The next step is to use this variable to follow a line.

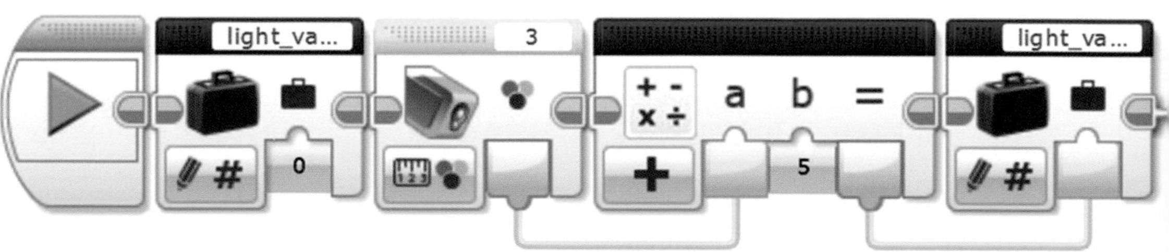

The darker your line is, the easier it will be for your robot to follow.

Look back at the looped part of your line-following program. The "Switch" icon is still set to compare against a value you measured and entered yourself. Instead, we want it to use the value from the variable we just made. Place a new "Variable" icon just inside the loop in front of the "Switch" icon. This time, change the option in the lower left corner of the icon to "Read numeric". Make sure the variable name is the same one you used for the other variable icons in the program. Connect a wire from the new "Variable" icon to the right tab on the "Switch" icon.

You have now created an automatic line-following program. You will not need to read the values from the line yourself. Your program will do it for you! Just make

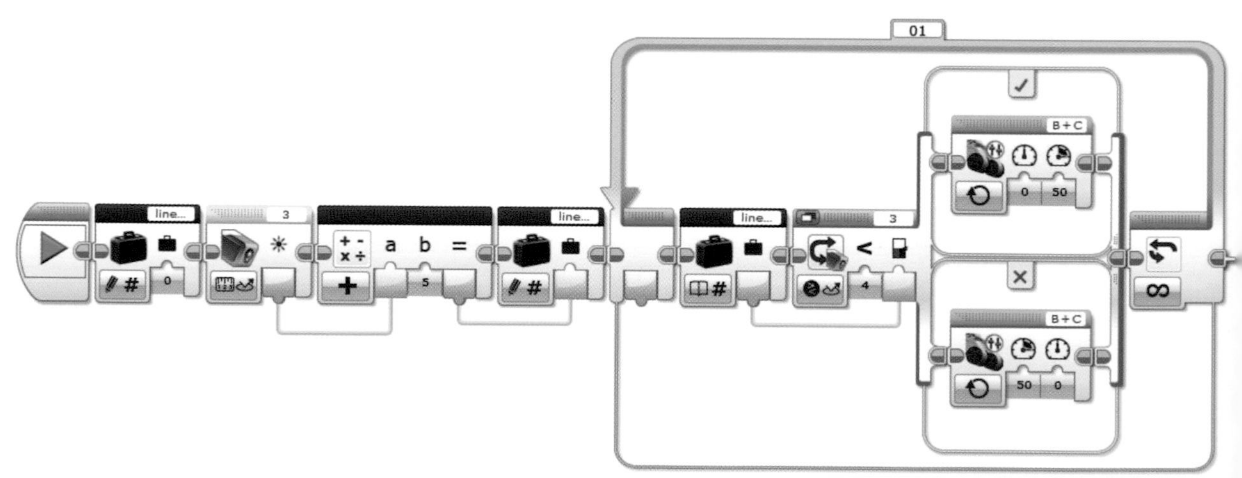

sure the light sensor is on the dark line when you start your robot. Also, remember that this only works if you have a dark line on a light background. What would you need to do if the line is light and the background is dark? There are actually two solutions. You could simply set your robot down to read the dark background instead of the line. The other way is to subtract 5 from your value instead of adding to it.

Chapter 3

Checking a Range

Sometimes when using the ultrasonic sensor, you might want to be within a range of an object rather than checking for a specific distance. For this example, we are going to assume that you want your robot to move until the ultrasonic sensor senses something within 3 to 10 inches (7.6 to 25.4 cm) in front of it. This will be a very simple program that teaches you how to use the range command.

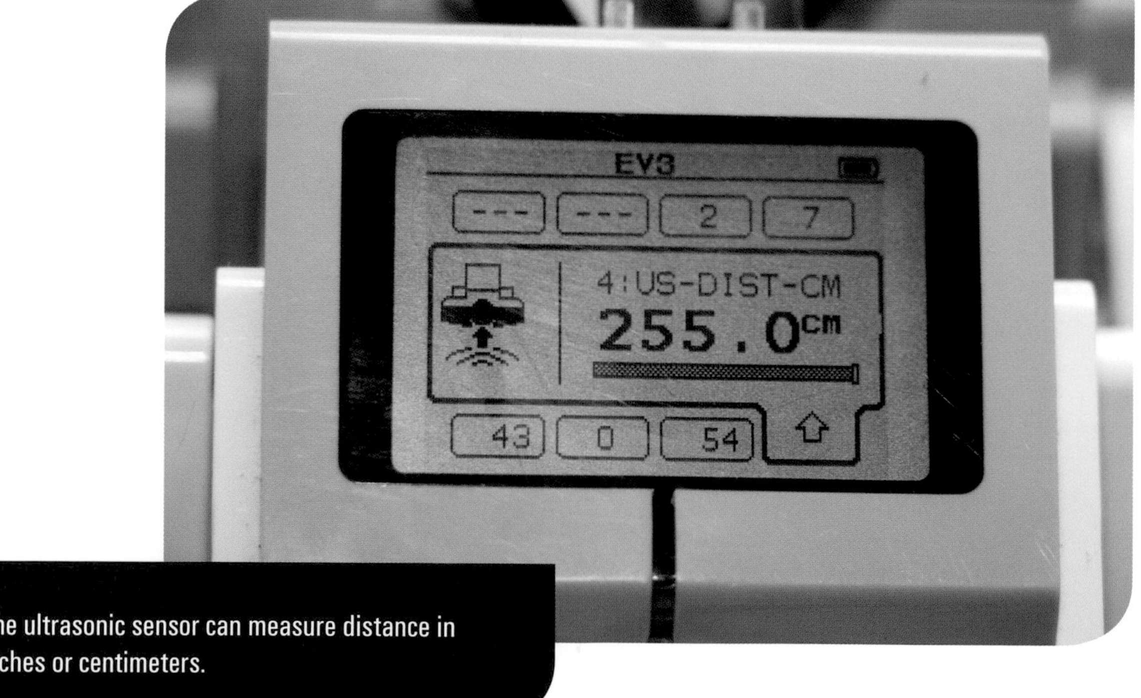

The ultrasonic sensor can measure distance in inches or centimeters.

How the Ultrasonic Sensor Works

Ultrasonic sensors produce sound waves that are outside the hearing range of human beings. These sound waves bounce off objects and return to the sensor. The sensor can then determine how far away the objects are. Ships use similar technology to measure the depth of the ocean and locate other objects underwater. Ultrasonic technology is used for medical purposes, too. For example, it can be used to create an ultrasound image of a baby inside a pregnant mother. It can also be used to diagnose conditions inside the body.

The "Range Command" icon is located under the red tab at the bottom of the screen. You can select either inside of a range or outside of a range by clicking the lower left part of the icon. In this case, you should select inside of a range. There are three tabs to the right of that section. The first tab is the value you will check the range against. The next two values are the limits of your range. To check a range from 3 to 10 inches (7.6 to 25.4 cm), the first tab value should be set to 3 and the second one should be set to 10. So far, though, you have not told it what value you want to check.

Go to the yellow tab and add an "Ultrasonic Sensor" icon to your program. Place it just before

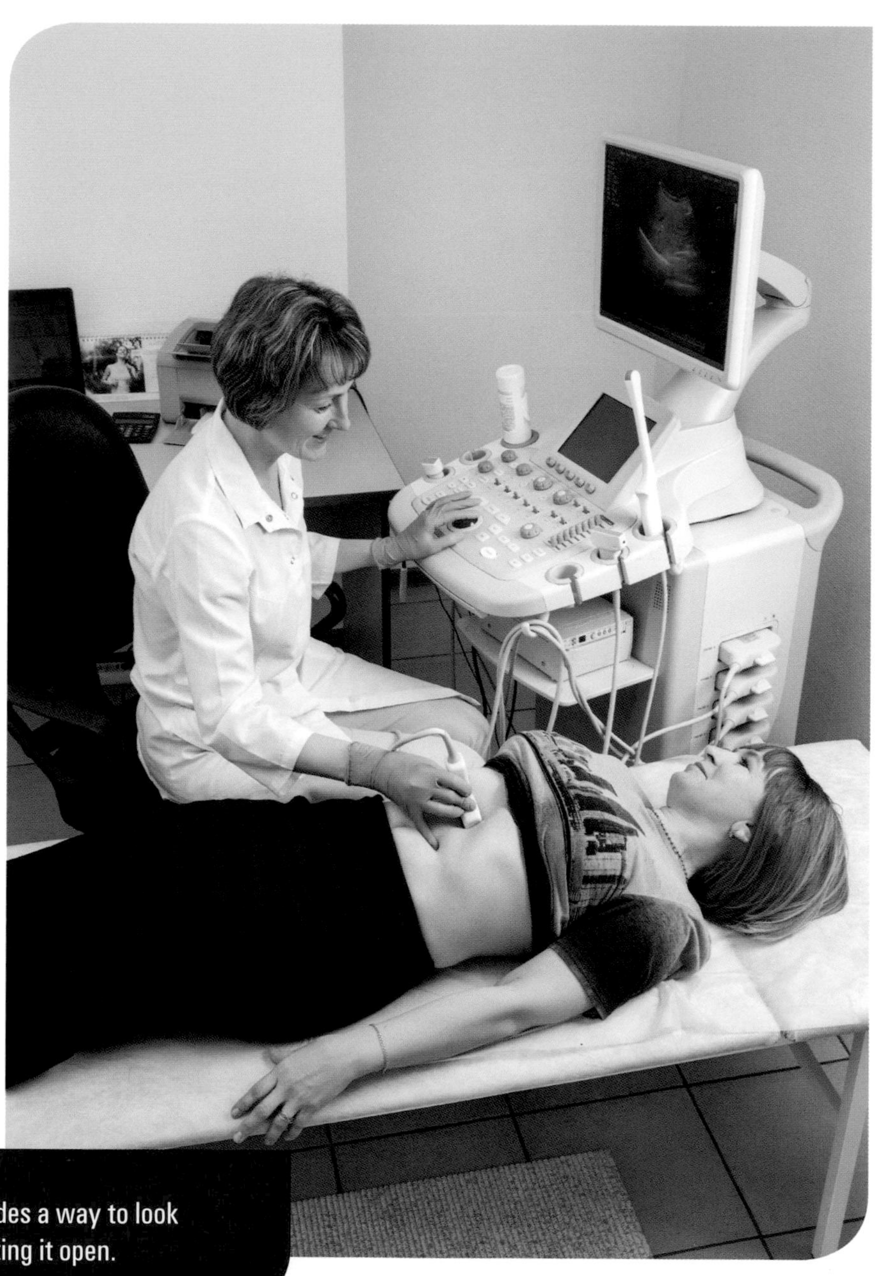

Ultrasonic technology provides a way to look inside the body without cutting it open.

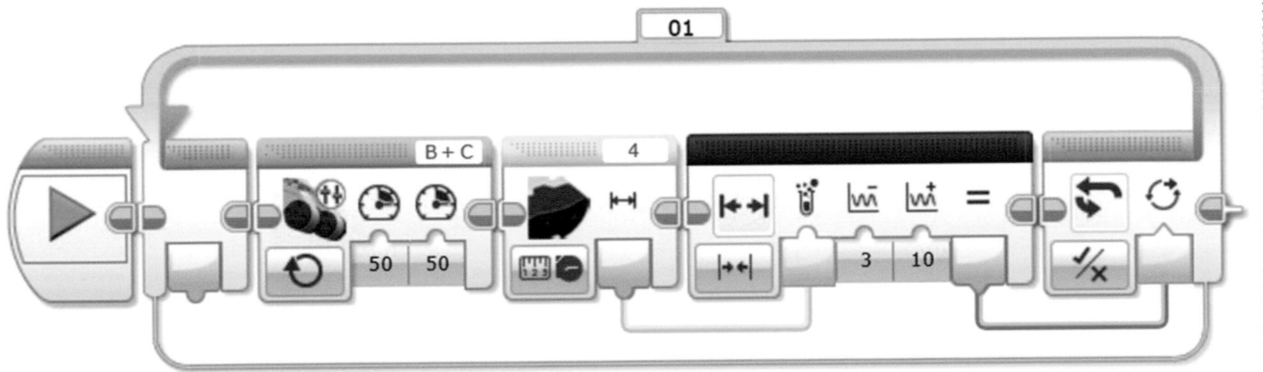

the "Range Command" icon. Set the sensor to measure distance in inches. Now pull a wire from the tab on the sensor icon and connect it to the tab labeled "value" on the range icon. With these two icons connected, your robot will read the value of the sensor and compare it to a range. The next step is to use this result to control something. In this case, you will use it to control a loop. Bring a "Loop" icon into your program and select the "Logic" option from the lower left. Connect a wire from the "=" tab on the range loop to the "until true" tab on the loop. Add a "Move Tank" icon, and you have a program that will

You can use the same robot here that you have used for previous activities in these books, or you can try building a new one.

drive forward until the ultrasonic sensor measures an object that is between 3 and 10 inches (7.6 and 25.4 cm) away.

Chapter 4

Detecting and Counting Lines

There are many interesting applications for the math icons in the EV3 software. Using the skills you have learned so far, you should be able to create a program that can count lines. How do you think this would work? Which sensors would you use? Before you read the rest of this chapter, try creating a line-counting program. Try to make the line count appear on the display screen of the EV3 unit. Take a look at the program later in this chapter if you need some hints. To test your program, use electrical tape to create some **parallel** lines on a piece of white poster board. Put different amounts of space between each line.

Did you get it to work? If not, don't worry. The program you developed could be correct in theory but will not work because of the speed of the robot.

When you ran your program, you might have seen a count that was much larger than the actual number of lines on your board. When the robot reaches a black line, it reads black just as you would expect. However, the light sensor can read extremely fast. Before the robot gets across the black line, it will read black many times. How do you think you can fix it so it will only count the line once?

There is more than one solution to this problem, but some are better than others. Let's try programming the robot to drive until it sees a line and counts the line, and then drives until it sees white before it starts counting again. This will make sure the robot only counts each black line once.

Start with a "Variable" icon set to 0. Name the variable "Line Count" or anything else that makes sense to you. Just be sure to use the same name for all the variable icons in the program.

Because you only need to set your variable to 0 once, leave this icon outside of a loop. And because your robot is always going to be moving, you can also turn the motors on a single time outside of the loop. The rest of the code should be inside of a loop. For now, you can make it an unlimited loop. Just remember to stop the robot once it has counted all the lines.

The next icon will be "Wait For". Select "Reflected Light" at the bottom left of the icon. Read the line value on your board and make the value here about 5 more. Now place a "Light Sensor" icon. Wire the output from that into the "a" tab of a "Math" icon. Put a "1" in the "b" tab. Be sure the bottom left is set to "add".

Add another "Variable" icon. Now wire the "=" tab on the "Math" icon to the input of the new variable. You also need to connect a second wire from the "=" tab to a "Display" icon. This will cause the total counted lines to appear on the display screen of the EV3. Once everything is in place, load the finished program onto your robot and test it out.

In this book, you have learned how to combine the basic programming skills that you already knew with some more advanced programming techniques. However, there are still many more things you can do

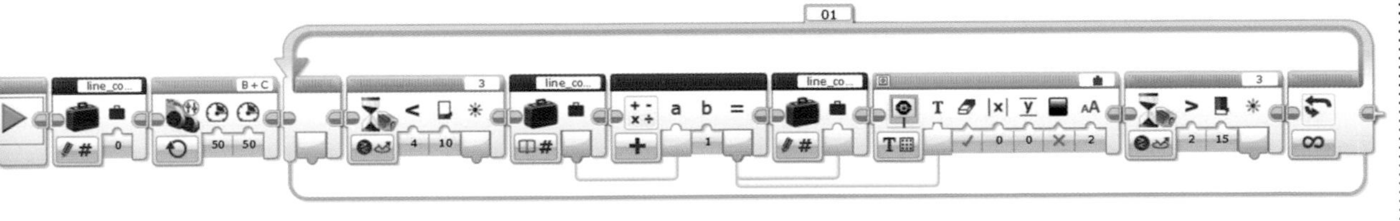

Starting From Zero

Do you remember adding a 0 variable to the start of your program in chapter 2? It is common practice for programmers to zero out all variables before using them, whether they are working with Mindstorms or any other programming language. This ensures that the value of a variable always starts at 0. Some programming languages automatically set variables to 0, but most programmers do not depend on this. The best way is always to set each variable to 0 before using it.

with your EV3. If you're ready for the next step, check out the next book in this series to learn more about some of the educational features of the EV3 and even more advanced programming.

What will you create next?

Glossary

executed (EK-suh-kyoo-tid) carried out a planned action

icons (EYE-kahnz) graphic symbols on a computer screen that represent programs, functions, or files

input (IN-put) information fed into a computer

output (OUT-put) information produced by a computer

parallel (PAR-uh-lel) staying the same distance from each other and never crossing or meeting

port (PORT) place on a computer that is designed for a particular kind of plug

troubleshoot (TRUHB-uhl-shoot) to try different things in an attempt to identify and solve a problem

variables (VAIR-ee-uh-buhlz) symbols that stand for numbers

Find Out More

BOOKS

Garber, Gary. *Instant Lego Mindstorms EV3*. Birmingham, UK: Packt Publishing, 2013.

Isogawa, Yoshihito. *The LEGO MINDSTORMS EV3 Idea Book: 181 Simple Machines and Clever Contraptions*. San Francisco: No Starch Press, 2015.

WEB SITE

Lego Mindstorms: Build a Robot

www.lego.com/en-us/mindstorms/build-a-robot
Check out instructions for building other Mindstorms robots.

Index

About the Author

Rena Hixon received a bachelor's degree in computer science from the University of Missouri–Rolla (now Missouri University of Science and Technology). She also earned a doctorate in electrical engineering from Wichita State University. She worked as a software design engineer for 11 years and has taught computer science classes at Wichita State for more than 13 years. In 2004, Rena and her husband started a Lego robotics club for homeschooled students. Its aim is to teach engineering principles, emphasizing math and science, to children. Rena has also taught her own Lego robotics camps for 12 years as well as camps at Missouri S&T for several years.